Down the River

Written by Paul Harrison

Collins

Down the river you can see a lock.

in

exit

LOCK25

A boat chugs near the river bank.

long boat

A kingfisher darts down to get a fish.

wings

Rivers join and get bigger.

reeds

soil

rushes

In the tunnel it is too dark to see.

light

Bigger boats join the river further down.

tugboat

sailboat

On the river

15

 After reading

Letters and Sounds: Phase 3

Word count: 55

Focus phonemes: /ai/ /ee/ /igh/ /oa/ /oo/ /ar/ /ur/ /ow/ /oi/ /ear/ /er/ /g/ gg /n/ nn

Common exception words: to, the, you

Curriculum links: Understanding the world: People and communities

Early learning goals: Understanding: answer "how" and "why" questions about their experiences and in response to stories or events; Reading: children use phonic knowledge to decode regular words and read them aloud accurately, read some common irregular words, demonstrate understanding when talking with others about what they have read

Developing fluency

- Your child may enjoy hearing you read the book.
- You could take turns to read a page. Model reading with lots of expression and encourage your child to do the same.

Phonic practice

- Practise reading words with more than one syllable together. Look at the word **river** on page 2. Say the word and clap each syllable as you do. Ask your child to sound talk and blend the letter sounds in each syllable "chunk": ri/ver.
- Then ask them to blend the sounds together.
- Do the same with the words **tunnel** and **kingfisher**.

Extending vocabulary

- Ask your child if they can tell you the opposite of each of the following words (antonyms):
  o near (*far*)
  o light (*dark*)
  o down (*up*)
  o long (*short*)